BULLYING

WITHDRAWN

A Parent's Guide

Jennifer
Thomson

First published in Great Britain in 2005 by
Need2Know
Remus House
Coltsfoot Drive
Peterborough
PE2 9JX
Telephone: 01733 898105
Fax: 01733 313524
Website: www.n2kbooks.com

Need2Know is an imprint of Forward Press Ltd.
Website: www.forwardpress.co.uk

SB ISBN 1-86144-044-8

Bullying: A Parent's Guide
Contents

Bullying: A Parent's Guide
Introduction

'Panarama: Why bullies win.'
'Former pupil sues over bullying.'
'School did nothing to stop bullying.'
'Suicide pact girl was bullied.'

It seems that you can't pick up a newspaper these days or turn on the TV without hearing about how the lives of children are being made a misery by bullies.

It seems that you can't pick up a newspaper these days or turn on the TV without hearing about how the lives of children are being made a misery by bullies. The headlines are everywhere. Alarmingly for parents often schools have been made aware of the bullying, and haven't always done everything in their power to stop it.

It's no wonder that so many parents are worried about bullying and have so many questions:

- How will I know if my child is being targeted?

- What can I do about the bullying if it is happening?

- Is my child's school fulfilling its obligations towards my child?

- How can I make my bullied child feel better about themselves?

It's time to sort out the facts from the fiction and to get to the crux of the matter.

School days are supposed to be the happiest of your life, but try telling that to the thousands of children who phone ChildLine and charities like it every year. They are being bullied and just can't take it anymore. For them, school is something that they dread. It's every parent's worst nightmare.

Could your child be one of them?

The good news is that bullying can be stopped. No one has to put up with it.

The government have recognised that bullying is such a big problem that, by law schools *must* have a bullying policy, and when you complain to them they have to do something about it. Not every parent is aware of a school's obligations to its pupils, so that will be covered in great detail in this book.

The damage that bullying causes can be severe. Bullying goes right to the core of a child's being and can ruin their chances of enjoying their time at school and getting the qualifications for the career that they want.

The damage that bullying causes can be severe. Bullying goes right to the core of a child's being and can ruin their chances of enjoying their time at school and getting the qualifications for the career that they want.

I know what it's like. As a bully survivor I've been there. I've had chewing gum stuck in my hair. I've had my head shoved down the toilet and flushed and been thrown into broken glass. I've had a boy come up to me on the school bus and stick his head in my face and spit *'ugly'* as every other kid watched. He was so close I could see the tiny scratch on his chin. I've cried myself to sleep at night and prayed that I wouldn't wake up again and have to go to school.

I never told anyone and it wasn't until I was older and the bullying seemed like a lifetime away that I realised that's where bullies get all their power from – their target suffering in silence. If no one knows anything is wrong how can they do anything about it?

That's why one of the main objectives of this book is to *get your child to confide in you*, because when you know something is wrong you can do something about it. The bully loses their power.

The natural response to the news that your child is being bullied is one of anger and of despair. It's often a case of *why did I not know it was happening, does my child not trust me enough to tell me?* As parents we feel that our children should be able to come to us with their problems and that we should be able to protect them against anything and everything. It comes as a great shock to us when we discover that we aren't superwoman or superman; that we can't keep them completely safe, and no, they don't always confide in us.

Then it's a case of *what can I do?*

The first thing anyone can do for a bullied child is to say *it's not your fault you're being bullied*. As a parent that is the most important thing you can say.

When I was being bullied over a series of years I believed that I was weak and a coward. I was too different. I didn't like the same stuff as other children. I smiled too much. I didn't smile enough. I bounced when I walked. (Crazy as it may sound I actually did believe that it was because I bounced when I walked.) Chances are that your child will feel that way too and it won't be a case of *there's something up with the bully*, it's *there's something up with me*. They need reassurance that is not so.

That's another aim of this book - to *stop your child from blaming themselves* and to *help build their self-esteem*, something that bullying eats away at.

There's another person who needs to stop blaming him or herself if their child is being bullied and that's you. No parent can be with his or her child 24 hours a day seven days a week. It just isn't possible. We can't all notice the warning signs especially when we don't even know what they are.

All we can do as parents is to equip ourselves with the knowledge and tools that we need to help our children in every way we can. That means getting clued up on the issues that affect them like bullying. It's time to tackle bullying . . .

All we can do as parents is to equip ourselves with the knowledge and tools that we need to help our children in every way we can . . . It's time to tackle bullying . . .

Chapter 1:
Bullying:
The Inside Story

Parents are quite rightly worried about the bullying culture that seems to be part and parcel of school life these days. Bullying is a problem that has been in the headlines constantly. The Prime Minister's barrister wife Cherie Blair has taken it to her heart. She chaired a ChildLine conference aimed at getting pupils and teachers round the table to share their strategies to end bullying in 2001. Such is the extent of the problem that there have even been calls to criminalise bullying. The government are just as concerned and since September 1999 every school must have an anti-bullying policy by law.

When you're a parent it can be easy to panic when you read these nightmare stories of bullying, that drove children to take their own lives, and to wonder if your child could be suffering at the hands of bullies as many children are. Are you worrying unnecessarily?

It's time to go beyond the headlines and to find out *just how widespread bullying is.*

Such is the extent of the problem that there have even been calls to criminalise bullying.

The Facts

Statistics show that most children will have some experience of bullying. That doesn't necessarily mean that they themselves will become a victim of a prolonged campaign by a bully or bullies, but sadly for many children it does as these facts show:

- According to BBC figures, eight out of ten children will be bullied at some time in their young lives.

- ChildLine recently announced a 42% rise in the total number of children counselled by the charity about bullying – the biggest annual increase in the charity's 18-year history. In the year April 2003 to March 2004 more than 31,000 young people spoke to a ChildLine counsellor about bullying – up from just over 21,000 during the previous 12 months.

- Bullying is the single biggest reason for children to call ChildLine and now accounts for one in four calls to the free, 24-hour helpline.

- Almost half of the children calling ChildLine in 1999, who were contemplating suicide, identified bullying as the prime cause.

- In a recent government survey a quarter of children questioned admitted that they were sometimes afraid to go to school because of bullying.

- In 1999 The Law Society of Scotland distributed leaflets throughout Scotland to inform children of their legal rights and telling them that they didn't have to put up with bullying.

- The government have recognised how bad the problem of bullying in schools has become, and recently gave schools in England and Wales new powers to exclude pupils who persistently bully.

... most children will have some experience of bullying. That doesn't necessarily mean that they themselves will become a victim of a prolonged campaign by a bully or bullies, but sadly for many children it does ...

What is Bullying?

Like everything a line has to be drawn. It's important we do this because quite often those who are being bullied are accused of being over sensitive. 'You can't take a joke,' is often the line that bullies will use to defend their actions. What we need to know as parents is when does the playful teasing that children do, cross over into something far more serious that we call bullying?

What is Bullying?

You could spend all day wracking your brains coming up with a definition that will fit perfectly and then someone else will come up with one that fits just as well. The general definition I like to use is -

Bullying is basically when someone does or says something deliberately intended to cause hurt or embarrassment to their target.

Sometimes children say things that aren't intended to hurt anyone, and although a bit insensitive and thoughtless, this would not be considered bullying. A clear distinction has to be made.

Types of Bullying

Bullying falls into two categories – physical and psychological. Bullying especially over a prolonged period of time often combines the two. For example children who are being called names, may also be kicked and punched, or have their heads pushed down the toilet.

There's a common misconception that bullying is only bullying when it involves violence or the threat of it, but psychological bullying can be just as traumatic as being assaulted. In fact, many children I talked to who were bullied said that it was the effect on their minds and the attack on their sense of self, that hurt more than the physical scars. The impact on their minds was also more difficult to recover from even long after the bullying had stopped.

Bullying is basically when someone does or says something deliberately intended to cause hurt or embarrassment to their target.

The Form Bullying Takes

'Our volunteer counsellors tell us that the calls they receive about bullying are some of the most painful they encounter,' says TV personality Esther Rantzen, ChildLine chairman.

Bullying has many guises. The behaviour of some pupils in our schools goes way beyond name-calling. Some children are physically assaulted and subjected to what can only be described as systematic psychological abuse.

The behaviour of some pupils in our schools goes way beyond name-calling. Some children are physically assaulted and subjected to what can only be described as systematic psychological abuse.

Mobile Phone Bullying

Sadly with new technology come new methods of bullies making other children's lives hell. There have been documented instances where children have been bullied by mobile phone. In extreme cases bullies have been caught using their mobile phones to send pictures of themselves attacking their victims to other bullies with some even being put onto websites. Email is also being used as a tool for bullies to threaten other children.

Simon, 14, was a victim of text bullying: 'I was getting hassled at school by a gang and they got a hold of my mobile number. They began texting me telling me that they were going to beat me up when they got me alone. Once they sent me a message saying that they were going to beat me up after school and steal all my clothes so I would have to go home naked. I got hit by a car as I tried to run away from them.'

Bullied Children's Stories

Sometimes with bullying something can trigger it off, although most bullies don't need any encouragement.

'We were playing another school for a netball trophy, I fluffed a shot and we lost. Since that day the other girls in the team have tormented me. They flooded my locker, spat in my face and stole my schoolbag. Once I tried to fight them and I ended up with a broken arm. I stopped going to school to escape them.'

Carly (15)

'I didn't know that this guy was going out with a girl in my group when I said I liked him. His girlfriend was furious and since then she and her mates have made my life hell. They've sent me to Coventry and when I walked past them they tripped me up. They send me emails telling me that today at school they're going to kill me.'

Sally (14)

'My family come from Bangladesh and I can honestly say that I've never experienced racism. That's until we moved and I started at a new school where I was the only Asian girl. The abuse started right away. They'd call me some awful things and tell me that I smelled as well as asking me racist questions like if my family cooked white people in a pot. Eventually I left the school and although I'm at another school where I'm the only Asian girl I don't have any problems and have lots of friends.'

Shoba (16)

Bullies Come in All Shapes and Sizes

It's not just other children who could be bullying your child. A teacher who seemed to take great delight from the fact that I had a speech impediment, which meant I couldn't pronounce the letter 'r' properly, used to pick on me. Guess who was always asked the solutions to the chemistry formulas where the answer was three? She'd get me to repeat it again and again until I was red in the face and felt like my head was going to explode. Thankfully the people in my class grew tired of it and she finally stopped.

Tasha, 16, was bullied by her elder brother: 'He'd wait 'til my mum was out and order me around. If I didn't do what I was told he'd hit me. I was too scared to tell my mum.'

Inside the Minds of the Bullies

I asked children who'd ever bullied and was surprised by what they said:

- Bullies are often children who have been bullied themselves, who like the sense of power they get when they turn the tables.

- They often have low self-esteem like their victims.

- Bullying gives them confidence.

- Some admit to bullying to get attention.

- Some bullies admit that they can't stop.

- Many bullies come from abusive homes and the only way that they know to interact and relate to others is through put-downs and physical violence.

- Many bullies started out as their victim's friend.

Where does the Bullying take Place?

The common misconception is that bullying always happens at school, but those school bullies are a crafty lot and are just as likely to do it outside school as much as in it. Danger areas can be anywhere. Your child's Saturday job, the library, even the bus stop. As parents we have to be alert.

The Effects of Bullying

Bullying damages children, so it's no wonder that its effects are wide and ranging:

- **Drug taking and binge drinking** – Victims may drink or take drugs to blot out the pain to help them cope. Trying to get over traumatic events is one of the prime causes of drug and alcohol addiction.

- **Playing truant from school** – School is where the bad things happen. Is it any wonder bullied children don't want to go there?

- **Stress** – Being bullied is a stressful experience putting victims on edge all the time and making them jumpy. The stress of anticipating the next attack can be worse than the actual bullying itself.

- **Depression** – Many children who are bullied end up having to be prescribed anti-depressants. This is perfectly common, but is not a long-term solution to the problem.

- **Panic attacks** – Anxiety is what causes the tightness in the chest and shortness of breath that characterises panic attacks. Breathing exercises can help this. So too can blowing into a brown paper bag.

- **Social phobias** – When a child is being bullied they may become terrified to go out and can become socially awkward.

- **Sleep disturbance** – Victims can suffer from nightmares and disturbing flashbacks.

The common misconception is that bullying always happens at school, but those school bullies are a crafty lot and are just as likely to do it outside school as much as in it.

- **Eating disorders** – In extreme cases children develop bulimia or anorexia. They can't control their lives, so they try and control the one aspect that they believe they can – what they eat. Once an eating disorder gets a grip of your child, even if the bullying was to stop, the anorexia or bulimia won't just go away. If you recognise your child here they need urgent medical help.

- **Self-harming** – This can be difficult for parents to understand. Why would a child who is being harmed by bullies resort to harming themselves? Self-harmers claim to get a kind of 'release' from hurting themselves, and harming themselves means they are in control. The most common method of self-harm is cutting, but it can also include doing things like burning yourself with cigarettes, sticking sharp objects in your arms and hitting your head repeatedly against the wall.

- **Suicide** – In extreme cases children can't take it anymore and decide to end their own lives. Most suicide attempts are cries for help, but some are genuine attempts to end their lives. The authors of *Bullycide; Death at Playtime*, a book, which looked at suicides caused by bullying, coined the term 'bullycide'.

Summing Up . . .

Maybe you (thankfully) had little or no firsthand experience of bullying before you picked up this book, but now that you know more about bullying you will be more in tune with what's happening out there and able to help your child if they become a target. The question you'll be asking now will be – *is my child being bullied?*

The chances are that if you picked up this book then the answer is yes, but if that is the case don't despair, there is a lot of help out there. Let's turn to the next chapter for a run through of the signs that will help you to realise if your suspicions are indeed correct.

Chapter 2:
Is My Child Being Bullied?

As a parent you are naturally protective towards your children and the thought that they are being bullied fills you with dread. The only thing that worries you more is the gnawing fear that they may be suffering in silence. If you think that your child is being bullied, how can you tell for sure? What are the signs to watch out for?

The good news is that there are signs that any child is being bullied, but they are not always that easy to spot so don't be too hard on yourself because you have failed to spot them. Many parents do. Besides, children can be good at hiding them, which makes seeing them extremely difficult. Plus there's the fact that children can start to behave very strangely as they near adolescence. It's called being a teenager!

. . . there are signs that any child is being bullied, but they are not always that easy to spot so don't be too hard on yourself because you have failed to spot them.

Signs to Look Out For:

- **They turn up with ripped or missing clothes.** This can be anything from a shirt that's torn to a scarf or jacket that's missing. Often children hide damaged clothes or dispose of them. It may be a good idea to ask them about that sweatshirt that they had on the other day that you can't find in the wash or those jeans that look like they have paint on them.

- **They don't want to go to school.** You may even suspect that they've played truant or faked an illness to get out of going. Ask them about it. Say 'Are you having problems at school and that's why you don't want to go?'

- **They become sullen and uncommunicative.** Okay, I know that could refer to most teenagers, but do they seem more unwilling to talk than usual? Do they tell you about their day, wait until you ask or snap at you when you do? If they wait on you asking and then grunt in reply or say nothing, is that a different response to normal? Spot the changes.

- **They become withdrawn.** They don't seem to like going out anymore and have few or no friends. They become extremely withdrawn locking themselves away in their room and putting music on so loud that they can't hear you.

- **Bruises and other signs of injury appear and there's no adequate explanation for them.** They may blame it on themselves saying they've been 'clumsy' or simply try to hide them.

- **They don't make eye contact when you talk to them and ask how they are doing.** If they say 'fine' or something to that effect yet avoid your gaze it may suggest they are lying to you. This may indicate that all is not well or may perhaps just be down to the them/us scenario that children have towards adults, especially when they become 13.

- **Suddenly not being friends with someone anymore and then getting evasive when you ask about it.** Former friends can become bullies.

- **Always speaking negatively about themselves.** For example calling themselves things like 'stupid' or 'useless' and never praising themselves or saying 'I'm good at that.'

- **They stop arguing with their brothers or sisters.** That's not typical sibling behaviour and may indicate that something is badly wrong.

- **They've gone from being fiercely independent to always needing you there.** They can't venture outside the home without you being with them. They have a need to feel protected.

- **They suffer from nightmares and panic attacks.** They may even start wetting the bed or suffering from nosebleeds.

- **They become depressed and can't muster any enthusiasm for anyone or anything.** They go off their food and nothing you do to try and cheer them up will raise so much as a smile, including things that are usually guaranteed to.

- **They may be accused of bullying themselves.** Many bullied children start bullying others. This may include siblings or their own friends.

- **They start taking a different route to school out of the blue.** They won't explain why, or they may ask you to drive them to lessons every day and then return to pick them up.

- **They change from being polite and well mannered into a monster who is aggressive, rude or disobedient.** This is something that has happened overnight and that can't be attributed to puberty. The reason they may be so angry is that they think that you should notice that they are being bullied.

- **They stop using their computer or mobile phone and are touchy about it when you ask them why.** They may be the victim of cyber bullying or text message bullying, two of the newest forms of bullying.

- **They develop a stammer or a nervous tic.** There was no evidence of these before. Something within them must have changed.

Why Children Hide Bullying

As parents we have to face up to the sad fact that as our children get older they are less likely to confide in us. That fact and the very nature of bullying and how it makes the victim feel combine to make many children feel that they can't tell on the bully. The tell-tale signs of bullying may be present and you may read them correctly, yet you may find that when you question your child about it you are met with complete silence or denial.

This is because children hide the fact they are being bullied for a variety of reasons:

- **Shame** – Children are ashamed to admit that they are being bullied. They don't want to be seen as weak or different or to draw attention to themselves. All the bullied child wants is the bullying to stop. That's why in a survey conducted by Kidscape and sponsored by the National Lottery they concluded that many adults still bear the scars of being bullied because they never felt able to tell anyone. Of course it should be the bully who is ashamed, but that's seldom, if ever, the case. So, the victim of bullying is left having to deal with not just the bullying, but also the shame that goes with it. I know I've been there myself. Maybe you have too.

The tell-tale signs of bullying may be present and you may read them correctly, yet you may find that when you question your child about it you are met with complete silence or denial.

- **Denial** – Some children just can't believe what is happening to them. One minute they're minding their own business and the next wham bam their life changes. They become someone who is being bullied. No wonder they enter a stage of denial, denying that they are being bullied even sometimes laughing off the bullying as something that they can put up with, when inside they are hurting.

- **They don't realise they are being bullied** - In some cases children may even be unsure that they are being bullied, something which sounds ridiculous, but you really have to experience bullying to be able to fully understand it.

- **Fear they won't be believed** – Well think about the way bullies operate, they try and keep what they are doing secret from the adults who can do something about it. Pupils aren't usually bullied inside the classroom in front of teachers, it's outside in the playground they are targeted away from the watchful eye of adults who will intervene. Children think that if they can't prove what's happening that they won't be believed.

- **Terror that the bullying won't stop** – 'If they (the bully) knows that I've snitched they'll make it even worse for me,' is a common reason why the bullied don't tell someone about what's happening to them. They feel that if they do, the abuse they are suffering will escalate.

- **They're worried they'll be treated like a grass** – What goes on in the world of your peers stays there. That seems to be one of the codes by which young people live by. To break that code by getting adults involved in their world is often seen as a complete no no. Do that and you could find yourself being ostracised.

- **They don't want to bother you** – The self-esteem of bullied children can often be so low because it's been eroded by the bullying. They genuinely feel that they shouldn't be wasting anyone's valuable time because they are not worth it. Perhaps deep down they think that they must deserve what is happening to them because unless they did, it wouldn't be happening. Maybe it's a case of they think you are too busy to hear about it.

- **Your attitude** – We have to be realistic here and face facts – sometimes as parents, we are not as approachable as we could be. One child I spoke to put up with a constant barrage of bullying for two years that included constant physical abuse, after he heard his father say that he should stand up for himself more. As a result of that comment he never did tell his parents about the hell he was going through. Thankfully for him they eventually found out and took the steps needed to get the harassment to stop. In his situation careless words uttered by his father could have prevented the bullying from ever coming out into the open.

- **They've admitted defeat** – The bullying may have been going on so long that they just can't see anyway or any day that it will ever come to an end. When children become this depressed it's vital that they get the urgent help that they need because they may be a suicide risk.

What your Child will say if they are being Bullied to Cover it Up

It's essential that you know when your child is not being truthful when you ask them if they are being bullied. Children can go to very great lengths to hide from adults the fact that they are being bullied. This may involve things like hiding ripped clothes, and claiming that bruises came from normal everyday activities, like playing football or larking about with their friends.

Here's a list of excuses that should set the alarm bells ringing straight away:

'I tore it playing football.'

'I lost/lent someone my lunch money.'

'I dropped it and it broke.'

'I got hit by the door/a football in PE. It was an accident.'

'I never liked that jacket so I gave it away.'

'I left my schoolbag on the bus.'

Children can go to very great lengths to hide from adults the fact that they are being bullied.

'I'm so clumsy. I'm always falling.' – The person who said this had her arm broken by a bully who then took a photo of her writhing in agony on her mobile phone.

'I swapped it with a kid at school.'

Why children find it so hard to talk about bullying

We've discussed why children hide the fact they are being bullied in the last chapter, but in order to fully understand why, who better to explain why they kept the bullying quiet than children and adults who were bullied.

'My parents were going through a bad divorce, the last thing they needed was me complicating things.'

Tess (13)

'I felt like I was the dog poo someone had just stood on.'

Clare (14)

'I started to believe that was just how things were. You got bullied or you bullied someone else.'

Ryan (15)

'My parents were going through a bad divorce, the last thing they needed was me complicating things.'

Tess (13)

'My mum's best friends with her (the bully) mum. I didn't think I'd be believed.'

Sean (14)

'They threatened to hurt my little sister if I told on them.'

Sophie (9)

Need2Know

Summing Up . . .

When it comes to bullying the best advice is to:

- Trust your instincts.

- Discuss your worries openly and honestly with your child no matter how much you feel like you are clutching at straws. What's the worst thing that could happen – that you're wrong? Is that so terrible?

It isn't always easy to tell if your child is being bullied when many children hide that fact. Most children don't just come right out with it. For more in depth advice about what to say to your child and how to make them stop blaming themselves for what's been happening to them read the next chapter.

Chapter 3:
Talking to
Your Child

You've already decided that your child is being bullied, the question now is how do you get them to open up about it so you can get the bullying to stop?

Getting bullied children to open up is a difficult process. They may have bottled it up for so long that they find it difficult to talk about it not necessarily because they don't want to, but perhaps they have difficulty articulating what's been happening. Maybe they feel scared to tell you because they worry about how you'll react. Perhaps they just don't want to be any trouble?

Bullies often threaten to hurt people close to their victims. In one shocking case I encountered, bullies threatened to kill and stuff a 13-year-old girl's beloved dog.

Getting Your Child to Open Up

If you want your child to feel able to talk to you there are certain things you should say and ones you should avoid.

Things to say:

- Be prepared. Know what you are going to say. The first words you utter when you talk to your child are critical. Make them the right ones.

- Use the Internet to look at information on bullying because it's an invaluable source of free information.

Be prepared. Know what you are going to say. The first words you utter when you talk to your child are critical. Make them the right ones.

- Pick a place where there are no interruptions. The best way to talk to your child is one on one. If there are other people around it will only make them self-conscious.

- Stress that what is happening to them is not their fault. The bullied usually think it is.

- Ensure they know that you will do everything that you can to get the bullying to stop.

- Get specific details from them about what's been happening. Did anyone witness any of these events? How did what happen make them feel? Who was involved?

- Discuss with them what action you can take. They have to know that the decision is a joint one. Ask them what they want you to do before deciding on a course of action, like contacting the school, or speaking to the bully or bullies' parents. Bullied children need to know that something will be done, and giving them a major role in the process will ensure they get some of the power they've had taken away by the bullies back.

- Tell them if you were bullied or anyone you know was, so that they can see that you emphasise with them and have an understanding of what it's like to be their age and have their problems.

- Be sensitive when asking them questions so that it doesn't come across as an interrogation.

Things to avoid:

- It's not easy, but don't get angry. The bully isn't in the room, but your child is and if you get angry they'll think you're angry with them, not the bully.

- Never suggest that it may be their fault. When 15-year-old Mary Jane told her mum about the bullying her mum responded with 'What did you do to cause that?' The blame for bullying has to be placed firmly at the bully's door because it is never the victim's fault.

- Don't tell them to stand up for themselves and ask why they didn't. It makes it sound like you are blaming them. Besides, maybe they did try to stand up for themselves and it backfired making them feel worse. Perhaps that's just not the kind of thing they can do because you brought them up to be a decent and compassionate human being, who respects others.

- Refrain from telling everyone about the bullying or you will make your child feel like everybody knows and is talking about him or her.

- Don't be angry with them because the bullying has been going on for so long and they haven't told you. This is a natural reaction not because you are angry with them, but because deep down you are angry with yourself. It has to be your fault they didn't feel able to talk to you. It's not, and blaming yourself and anyone other than the bully is pointless.

- Threaten the bullies or their parents with violence. That's the last thing you should do. Of course you're angry, but violence never solved anything.

- Make promises that you can't keep, for example say you'll take them out of school if need be and teach them at home. When you have no intention of doing that it will destroy their trust.

- On no account should you promise to keep what your child has told you confidential. This can be difficult for a parent to do especially when your child is so obviously upset, but there's no way you can take action if you keep what they have told you to yourself.

- Whatever you do, do not be tempted to take your child out of school and take them away on holiday to give them a break. The bullying problem has to be sorted out now as a matter of great urgency. Leave it until later and your child will only worry.

Don't tell them to stand up for themselves and ask why they didn't. It makes it sound like you are blaming them.

The Right Questions to Ask

You've ascertained that the bullying is going on, but what do you need to know now?

- How long this has been going on?

- Who was involved?

- Can they name names?

- What exactly has been happening? Does the bullying involve things like physical violence or theft of property? This may come in useful if you need to go to the police.

- Were there any witnesses or was it caught on CCTV?

- Did they tell anyone? This can include anyone from friends to teachers.

- Have they got any records of the bullying? For instance did they write about it in their diary or in a note to a friend? A heart rendering record of the bullying can come in handy when it comes to approaching the school.

- Do they have any injuries now? Perhaps they need medical help. If they do have injuries take photographs of them and find out exactly how they got them. Documenting evidence in this way will come in useful later.

- Do they feel able to talk to a teacher about the torment they've suffered?

. . . talking to your child about bullying may not be that easy. You need to pick your moment and your approach carefully.

Getting Your Child to Open Up

In view of all the things we've discussed talking to your child about bullying may not be that easy. You need to pick your moment and your approach carefully. Here are some suggested scenarios for you to try:

Scenario 1 - Have a general 'we're here for you' talk

Sometimes our children need to be reminded just how much we love them. Sit down with your son or daughter and tell them. Take this as an opportunity to ask them if anything is troubling them. Some children never tell you about bullying because they just don't know how to pick the right time.

Scenario 2 - Bringing up a particular incident

Sometimes it's best not to pussyfoot around the issue and to actually come out and ask them if they are being bullied. Don't do this when they are distracted by the TV or are listening to music. Don't do it in front of their siblings. The best place to do this is probably in their bedroom or in the garden where you won't be disturbed and can have a real heart to heart. Admit that you are worried that they may be getting bullied at school and try and gauge their reaction to see if it confirms it even if their words don't.

Scenario 3 - The day out in a relaxed atmosphere

A change of scenery can work wonders. Try taking your child out somewhere you know that they will enjoy. This can be anywhere. For younger children try an amusement park, a trip to the beach, skating rink or local McDonalds. For older children take them to a venue of their choice, or treat them to something you know they'd like. Taking them out of their home environment will allow them to relax, making them more liable to open up to you about what's been happening.

Scenario 4 – Ask someone else to talk to your child

There are times when we have to step aside as parents and enlist other people's help and this may be the occasion for that. If you are worried that they won't be able to open up to you about the bullying then ask someone who is close to them to speak to them. This can be their grandmother, auntie, big sister or older brother – someone who they relate well to. What's important is that your child admits they are being bullied, not whom they actually admit that to.

Glued Mouth Syndrome

There is a strong chance that despite your best efforts you won't be able to get them to speak to you. You can't force them to admit to what's been happening, so if your initial attempt to get it out of your child fails try and try again. Admitting you're being bullied isn't easy. It takes a lot of courage. Tell them that. Make sure they know they can come to you at any time. Also suggest that if they are worried about anything they can write you a letter. Sometimes it can be easier to write it down.

Tip - It's good for the communication between you and your child if you set aside a regular time to chat to them about things. That way they will know they can come to you about anything.

What Your Child is Likely to Say

Your child may try and play down the bullying. They may blame themselves or claim that it's stopped. That's typical of the way bullied children behave.

They are also likely to have questions for you that you will need to answer the best you can. They need that reassurance. Here are some of the most likely ones so that you can come up with some answers before you speak to them.

- Why me? - This is one of the most common questions that the bullied child asks. The child needs to know that it isn't their fault.

- Why do bullies do it? - They need to understand why people can be so cruel.

- Did I do something to deserve it? - The victim feels like they've brought it upon themselves in some way. This is your opportunity to tell them that's not true loud and clear.

- Can you get it to stop? – They need reassurance here that the bullying will stop.

- Is this happening because no one likes me? - Stress that it isn't.

- Will I always feel as bad as this? - Be positive about the bullying finally stopping. Tell them that once the bullying ends they will return to their happy old self. Talk about something good that's happening in the future like a holiday or family party.

- Were you bullied? - A little white lie may not go amiss here. Sometimes as parents we have to do that so that our children feel as though we can relate to them.

'He was Bullied too You Know!'

Knowing that stars were bullied too and still managed to come out the other side and be a success, can make those who've been bullied feel better about themselves and what has happened to them. Dropping their names into the conversation when talking about bullying with your child can make them more likely to admit they've been bullied if they know that celebrities have suffered too.

- Did you know for example that Tom Cruise was bullied because he was dyslexic and was a 'weedy kid?'

- Gareth Gates was bullied because of his stammer.

- David Beckham was also targeted at school and claims he was the last one to be picked for the school football team.

- Beautiful actress Michelle Pfeiffer was teased about her looks especially her lips and was nicknamed 'Michelle Mudturtle' by schoolmates. She used to run home crying.

- Diva Whitney Houston also used to face a barrage of insults because of the way she looked.

- Former Westlife star Brian McFadden used to face jeers of 'Fat Boy' and 'Chunk' at school.

- Oscar nominated Hollywood actress Samantha Morton was in and out of care homes when she was a child and was mercilessly bullied by other children. She once found broken glass and excrement in her bed and a teddy and diary her mother had given her were burnt.

Many parents say that they knew there was something wrong at a very early age...

Summing Up . . .

Finding out your child is being bullied is a very distressing and difficult time. First and foremost they need to know that it is not their fault. Too many bullied children blame themselves.

It's imperative that they are also aware that you will do everything you can to get the bullying to stop.

Most of all, after discussing what's been happening with you, your child will no longer feel alone. A problem shared is a problem halved and in the case of bullying - solvable.

Chapter 4:
Why My Child?

Discovering that your child is being bullied can be difficult for a parent to come to terms with. Why is it happening to my child? Am I to blame? Did I not raise them right? Are my parenting skills at the root of what's been happening? You will ask yourself these questions and more as you try to make sense of it all.

It's only natural that parents should feel that way. No matter how grown up and independent our children get they are still our babies and we feel that we should be able to protect them from anything. It's a hard blow for any parent to take when we realise that we can't. Ultimately no parent can, but that doesn't stop us from feeling that we should be able to. It's one of the joys of being a parent.

So, why the blame game?

Am I to Blame?

In the case of bullying we fear that we may have done something to make them a target for bullies. Perhaps we didn't equip them with the necessary social skills? Maybe we didn't give them the toughness that they need to cope with difficult situations and people. Terrible parents that we are, bringing up decent individuals instead of insensitive morons.

Not that it's any consolation, but your child will be blaming themselves too, because ultimately the main problem with bullying is that everyone blames themselves for it except for the ones causing all the trouble - the bullies.

. . . the main problem with bullying is that everyone blames themselves for it except for the ones causing all the trouble - the bullies.

Why Your Child Being Bullied isn't Your Fault

One of the most common myths of all about bullying is that it's the fault of parents who have made their children targets. Perhaps the parent was bullied themselves and fears that they have passed on a bullying gene or a mode of behaviour that makes their offspring behave in a certain way that attracts bullying. Maybe it's because they haven't bought their child the same kind of fancy trainers that everyone else is wearing. Or it could even be that their child has been brought up to be gentle and kind and not tough.

The truth is of course is that *the only person to blame is the bully themselves* and any adult who knowingly allows them to carry on with their behaviour.

Shattering the Myths About Bullying

It's easy to be sucked into the myths that surround bullying and to treat them as fact. In order to understand the nature of the beast we are dealing with here we have to examine them and the rationale behind them and then smash them to smithereens:

'My child must have done something that triggered the bullying.'

The reasoning: Nothing happens for no reason. This one really suits the bullies because it exonerates them of all blame. It's not their fault. It's the children they pick on.

False - If someone gets mugged you don't turn round and say they deserved it, it's the way they dangled their purse about, dared to wear that gold necklace, thought that they could have that £400 mobile phone. Bullying is a crime and the victims are never to be blamed. Doing that just falls into the bullies' hands.

Need2Know

'Bullying is just part of growing up.'

The reasoning: Everybody gets bullied. It just happens. Bad things do.

False - That may be a sad reality for many children but that doesn't make it right or acceptable. Every child has a right to live in a nurturing environment without fear where they can enjoy their childhood and grow into well-rounded adults.

Bullying forces children to live in fear and can squash their potential as well as changing their character irrevocably. How is any of that natural and normal? Childhood is meant to be a carefree time not a fearful one.

'Bullying toughens kids up.'

The Reasoning: This myth seems to imply that it's an important part of a child's development to be bullied. That children need to encounter and face up to the bullies of this world so that they will be tough enough to know how to deal with them when they are adults.

False - There's overwhelming evidence to suggest that bullying weakens people instead of toughening them up. Why else would adults still speak with terror of the bullying they suffered when they were at school? The bullying has had such a profound and often devastating effect on them and the effects still linger even today when the bullying has long since stopped.

I know that from my own bitter experience. Even today I can't pass a gang of teenage boys without breaking out into a cold sweat because it was a group like that who terrorised me sixteen years ago.

'This is my fault because I'm never there.'

The reasoning: It's the children of negligent parents who get bullied.

False - These days a heap of blame seem to get dumped at the doors of parents who have to work to ensure their children are fed and clothed, so why shouldn't it be the case with bullying?

Children from all kinds of families get bullied. You could be a stay at home parent, the kind who makes their child a packed lunch and sees them off to school every day and your son or daughter may still end up getting bullied. Being bullied has nothing to do with whether you are there for your child 24 hours a day or only spend a couple of hours with them if you are lucky. Single parent families or families where both parents work – bullies don't discriminate. Besides no parent can be with their child every minute of every day, which is what you would have to do to ensure they don't get bullied.

'Bullying is something that has always gone on, that will always go on and there's nothing we can do about it.'

The reasoning: Things don't change.

False - This is the kind of defeatist attitude that allows bullying to thrive. Instead of trying to stop it people just shrug their shoulders and say 'There's nothing we can do.' If everybody did that what would happen? Bullies would just be left to get on with it and their victims left to suffer usually in silence. Is that what people want? I think we all know that it's not.

Bad things happen because people stand by and do nothing. Who wants to be one of those people?

The apathetic attitude to bullying could just as well be applied to say global warming. Why bother trying to reverse it? We want to try because even though we face an uphill struggle it's human nature to want to right wrongs. It's what makes us marvellous human beings instead of robots who merely accept things.

Just remember that if every person does their bit to stop bullying it will eventually become one of those awful things like children being sent to work houses in Victorian times that people talk about in hushed tones, disgusted that it ever happened in the first place.

'If my child just stood up to the bully the bullying would stop.'

The reasoning: Bullies are looking for a sign of weakness and when they find it that's when they latch onto their prey. By that same rationale, if a man gets mugged in the street by two assailants it would be his fault not his attackers. Well, he should have told the muggers to take a hike surely?

False - Often this is the stuff of folklore. Not all bullies back down when challenged because the very nature of bullying means that quite often bullies surround themselves with their friends who are often bullies too. This means that a child could find themselves outnumbered. Bullying isn't one on one; it's usually the cowardly bully and their mates. The victim is the person who is often alone.

'If my kid punched the bully on the nose that would be the perfect solution.'

The reasoning: The bully is looking for weakness. Punch him on the nose and he will realise your child isn't weak - he is.

False - Maybe it would be if the bullying was one on one, but violence is not the answer to anything. What kind of message does it is send out to children when anyone suggests that it is? Inevitably all it does is leads to trouble.

In one case I found out through my research Alistair* was threatened with a shovel by the teenager who had been bullying him for months. He grabbed the shovel from him and in the tussle ended up knocking him flying. Guess who ended up being cautioned by police?

Assault is a crime and bullies are often the type of people who will be perfectly happy to bully a smaller child but if they happened to get hurt they would be pretty quick in getting the police involved. Do you want your child to have a criminal record when it's their bully who should have one?

Bullying isn't one on one; it's usually the cowardly bully and their mates. The victim is the person who is often alone.

*Name has been changed.

'I have raised a weak child because only weak people get bullied.'

The reasoning: Bullies only pick on those they see as weak.

False - Terrible parent that you are you have raised a child who respects others and doesn't bully other children. Research shows that they are the children most likely to get bullied. How can you look in the mirror?

The stark fact is that children are bullied for all sorts of reasons. Maybe it's the colour of their skin, their weight (too skinny or overweight), their religion, them not wearing 'the right trainers' or the fact that they are popular/smart/beautiful/funny/have a Roman nose.

'This is my fault because I was bullied at school too.'

The reasoning: I have turned my child into a miniature version of me, a victim.

False – It's understandable that discovering the same terrible, damaging thing that happened to you is also happening to your child will bring back painful memories and feelings that you would rather forget. That doesn't mean that you are correct when you blame yourself for the bullying. Most children will encounter bullying at some stage. With those kind of odds it's no surprise that your child has been targeted.

'I was bullied at school too and it never did me any harm, so my child's just being over sensitive.'

The reasoning: This happened to me. I got over it.

False - Have you ever heard the phrase different strokes for different folks? People react to bullying differently and there are different degrees of bullying. Besides, the bullying that goes on now may be different to what you suffered. There's much evidence to suggest that nowadays bullies are more prone to using physical violence and the everyday use of mobile phones and computers means that they have new ways of tormenting their victims.

Until you are in someone's shoes, including your own child's it's impossible for you to know how the bullying makes them feel and how severe it actually is.

Until you are in someone's shoes, including your own child's it's impossible for you to know how the bullying makes them feel and how severe it actually is.

'If I move my child to another school that will definitely solve the problem.'

The reasoning: I can make the problem go away by moving my child.

False - Yes this could work, but what happens if your child is targeted again at their new school? What then? Do you move them to another school and one after that? Bullying has to be dealt with, not sidestepped.

As well as dealing with the bullying you also have to try and counteract the effects on your child's self-esteem. Chapter 9 will offer ways to help you to do that.

Summing Up . . .

You find out that your child is being bullied and you ask your friends if it's happened to their children and they say no. You have a right to ask yourself *why is it happening to my child?* Who wouldn't ask that question?

The simple fact is that what's happening is not your fault or your child's as debunking the myths that hang around bullying prove.

Chapter 5:
How to Prevent Your Child from Getting Bullied

'Bullying is just a fact of life and nothing can be done about it.'

'Bullying will always go on.'

'Children are either bullies or they're bullied.'

Sadly there are people who genuinely believe those statements to be true. But they're wrong. There are steps that you and your child can take to lessen their chance of getting bullied. The good news is that they can be used in conjunction with other roads parents go down to stop bullying including going to your child's school if they are being picked on. Let's call it bully avoidance.

Who is the Bully?

Before we try and adopt some bully avoidance strategies we first have to know what we are dealing with here. We have to build a profile of the bully. Who are they and who are they most likely to pick on? How do they operate? Most importantly, how can that help you to keep your child free of harm?

Not every bully is the same but they tend to share the same characteristics:

- Bullies pick on children who are different; often it is these very qualities that make some children susceptible to bullies which are also the ones that make them special. Bullies can be jealous of their victims.

- Bullies pick on children who lack confidence. A child who walks about looking down at their feet is more likely to be bullied than one who walks with their head held high because they ooze confidence.

- Bullies usually pick on children who are on their own because they are cowards. If they thought that the tables could be turned on them they wouldn't bully anyone.

- Bullies tend to do it in groups usually of friends or other victims because they like an audience. This also gives them back up and strength of numbers. Bullies only bully when they know that they can get away with it.

- Bullies are usually physically stronger than the person they are bullying and are often older. They don't want to take the chance of someone they're taunting belting them. This is usually why parents urging their child to 'just hit him/her back' isn't an option like violence never should be.

- They have a distinct lack of sympathy for their victim and can't put themselves in their shoes or anyone else's for that matter. They often have trouble relating to anyone else.

- Many bullies come from homes where violence is used as a means to get what they want. Bullying can be a learned behaviour, which means that it can also be unlearned.

What You can do to Prevent Your Child from being Bullied

As parents there are things that we can do to help our children especially now we know how most bullies operate. These methods won't completely rule out the chance of your child being bullied, but what they will do is greatly cut down the opportunities for the bullying to take place.

Strategy 1 - Encourage your child to be themselves

Being an individual can lead to children being singled out because they are different, but it will give them the confidence that repels bullies, not attract them.

Achieving this: Don't automatically buy them things that other children their age are getting. Ask them what they like. What they want. Let them develop their own likes and dislikes. If they take up an unusual hobby encourage them. Take an active interest. Let them be their own person and to feel good about being that person.

Strategy 2 - Encourage your child to socialise

No child deserves to be bullied, but there are certain character traits that make some children more susceptible to bullying. The main one is social awkwardness. Other children may pick up on this and that's when the trouble can start. That's why it's important that children make friends. New friends can give children, especially ones who've been bullied a new lease of life.

Achieving this:

- Try inviting some of their friends around and let them know that they are always welcome.

- Within reason allow your child to accept invitations to socialise with their friends.

- If your friends have children encourage them to socialise with yours.

- Encourage your child to participate in physical activities even if they are reluctant. Physical exercise is good for a child's confidence and there's always at least one sport that even a non-sporty child can enjoy. They don't have to be good at it.

No child deserves to be bullied, but there are certain character traits that make some children more susceptible to bullying.

Strategy 3 - Have your very own bully drill

If your child feels that they are in a situation that they can't handle say they are being chased by bullies, decide on a safe place that they can go to like a shop or a neighbour's house. This will give them a safety net and stop them feeling the loneliness that many bullied children feel because they have no one to turn to at the very point where they need it most.

Achieving this: Discuss this with them beforehand (try and be light hearted about it not alarmist) and give them a number of an available adult they can call to come and get them.

Strategy 4 - Raise an independent child

Having an independent child means having a confident child and that will make them less likely to be bullied.

It's difficult in this day and age for parents to feel safe about letting their children out of their sight, but they've got to learn to fly sometime. We did it. Having an independent child means having a confident child and that will make them less likely to be bullied.

Achieving this:

- If they are old enough let them go places with their friends that they usually go with you, say in to town.

- If you pick them up from school then let them take the bus for a change and give them money to go to McDonalds with their friends.

- Give them some responsibility. This will show that you have faith in them and trust them. This can be anything from letting them look after a pet to laying the table at home.

Strategy 5 - Ensure your child knows how to report incidents of bullying

One teacher I spoke to about bullying said that the reason it's such a big problem is that often the victims aren't very coherent or detailed when it comes to telling adults about what's happened to them. Every incidence of bullying has to be reported as succinctly as possible in order for something to be done about it.

Achieving this:

Teach your child that any report of bullying should include:

1. What happened.

2. Where and when did this happen.

3. Who did what.

4. Who else saw what happened.

5. What they did.

6. How what happened made them feel.

Strategy 6 - Educate your child about bullying and bullies

I know from my own bitter experience that when you are being bullied you are caught in a vicious circle of doubt and you believe that you have done something to merit what is happening to you. What you need is for someone to say that what's happened is not your fault and that it won't go on forever.

Achieving this:

- Tell them that bullying is never the victim's fault; it's the bully who is in the wrong and that if you found out they were being bullied you would never blame them.

- Make sure they know that you regard bullies as cowards and they are the ones who should be ashamed, not the people they pick on.

- Stress that bullying can be stopped.

- Assure them that you will do everything that you can to stop them from being bullied including the worst case scenario of taking them out of school if necessary, but only if you really mean it.

. . . when you are being bullied you are caught in a vicious circle of doubt and you believe that you have done something to merit what is happening to you.

Strategy 7 - Make sure that your child knows the importance of body language

There's something that I call the 'victim' stance. It's when your shoulders are hunched, your head is down and you avoid making any eye contact. Bullies love this stance. You want your child to walk in a confident manner even if they don't feel confident.

Achieving this: Teach them some confident body language. Get them to practice in front of a mirror.

If this doesn't do the trick try sending them to an Alexander Technique teacher. Actors go to these specialists who teach people how to achieve the right posture. See Help List at back of book for contact details.

Strategy 8 - Make sure that your child has a safe and nurturing environment at home

This will help give them more confidence and also make them feel more able to tell you if they are being bullied.

The confidence that bullies have is derived mainly from the fact that in most cases they know that their victim won't tell. By creating a home life where you're child feels that they can tell you anything, you shift the power balance in you child's favour.

Achieving this:

- Talk with your child, not at them. This way they are more likely to come to you when they have a problem.

- Try and stay calm at all times and cut down the raising of your voice to a minimum. No one gets their point across by shouting, but everyone does it.

- If you have a problem discuss it with them don't shout.

- Be interested in your child and their life. Ask them what they did in school that day. Spend time with them even if it's only to watch a TV programme.

- If they do something well tell them. Children need praise to feel good about themselves.

What Your Child Can Do

No child could completely bully proof their life unless they stayed in all day and hid under the duvet, but there are things that children can do to limit their chance of being bullied.

Children should:

- Never give out their phone number to anyone except their closest friends. Text bullying is sadly a new trend. Jane, one 14-year-old I spoke to was hounded by bullies who sent her cruel text messages saying how they were going to 'get her' and 'set fire to her hair.'

- Try and be with a group of friends at all times. Bullies tend to hang about in gangs and pick on children on their own. They're too cowardly to target whole groups of people because there's a chance that they will be the ones made to look stupid.

- Leave classes with friends or with a teacher. This is especially pertinent if your child has been the target of bullies in the past.

- Avoid places where bullies are likely to be.

- Never take expensive things to school. Jealously may attract bullies.

- Ask bullies to repeat what they just said (bullies hate this). Some victims of bullying say that it helps if they have replies ready to regular taunts because the bully isn't expecting it.

- Try to act more confident – even if they don't feel it.

No child could completely bully proof their life unless they stayed in all day and hid under the duvet, but there are things that children can do to limit their chance of being bullied.

What if My Child is the Bully?

Not every child who is involved in bullying is on the receiving side. There are those who are the ones dishing it out. This may come as a shock to some parents when they discover that their child is a bully.

How to Stop Your Child Bullying

- Try and get to the root of why they do it. Were they bullied themselves and they think that by bullying others they will get back the power that they lost? Have they learnt this behaviour in the home? Maybe you should be looking at how you behave. Do you adopt bullying behaviour? Be honest. Often bullies learn the behaviour from family members. If the behaviour is uncharacteristic, could something be worrying them and that's why they are lashing out?

- Make sure that they know how much you disapprove of their behaviour, but don't say that you're ashamed of them or that you're disowning them even if you feel that way. They've got to know that it's their behaviour you disapprove of - not them. They need an incentive to change.

- Work out a way for them to stop bullying. Maybe they think that aggression is the best way to deal with any kind of conflict. Teach them other ways.

- Come up with a suitable way that they can make amends for the bullying. This could be something as simple as apologising to their victim or writing an essay to be read out in front of the class.

- Look at how they resolve conflicts within the home. This can give you a clue as to how they behave when they're away from your scrutiny.

- Get them to emphasise with their victim. Bullies tend to lack empathy and this is why they continue to bully. Try role-playing where you give them a taster of what it's like to be on the receiving end for a change.

. . . don't say that you're ashamed of them or that you're disowning them even if you feel that way. They've got to know that it's their behaviour you disapprove of - not them.

Need2Know

Summing Up . . .

- Bullying doesn't have to be a fact of life.

- To prevent our children from being bullied we have to be aware of how the bully behaves and come up with strategies to counteract that.

- There are things that our children can do to prevent becoming victims like ensuring they are always with friends, never giving out their phone number and being confident.

- Bullying may be a problem for your child in a different way to the way you might think. They might be the one doing the bullying.

Chapter 6:
Going to the School

You find out that your child is being bullied at school and all guns blazing you want to march right down there and give them what for. A perfectly natural reaction, but how many parents do you think have done that and come away feeling that they've been brushed aside or feeing foolish because they haven't gone to the school with the facts that they need to get something done? Too many unfortunately.

Before you even think about going to the school you need to be prepared: to know you and your child's rights inside out. Go armed with the necessary information at your disposal and you have more chance of the school taking the necessary action to stop the bullying dead in its tracks. Don't go prepared and you face making it a long drawn out process that will infuriate you and cause further damage to the injured party – your child.

Why the School should be Your First Port of Call

As parents are legally obligated to send their children to school or to educate them at home, schools are regarded as being in *loco parentis**. Whilst your child is at school they are affectively the ones who are deputising for you, the absent parent. Schools have a duty of care to your child and are obligated to provide children with a safe learning environment. Bullying infringes upon that duty.

In addition *by law schools must have a policy on bullying*, which clearly states their responsibilities and the sanctions they will take to deal with bullying if and when it arises.

Before you even think about going to the school you need to be prepared: to know you and your child's rights inside out.

* This fact was established by the Court of Appeal, who decreed that the school headteacher stands in loco parentis (in place of the parents).

What Schools Aren't Responsible For

Before you go to the school all pumped up demanding to know what they are going to do about your son or daughter being bullied there are a two things that you need to know.

Fact One – Schools are not deemed to be responsible for bullying that goes on outside the school gates.

This was the surprise High Court ruling in 1990 in a case brought by Leah Bradford-Smart who claimed she'd suffered 'persistent and prolonged bullying' for three years and sought damages in court. Her lawyer argued that the school still had a duty of care to pupils outside the gates, but the judge decided otherwise.

The minute the school are made aware of it and have been given enough time to act they are liable.

In most cases this verdict won't harm your case against the bully because in the majority of incidences the actual harassment is likely to happen within the school grounds at least at some point.

If your child is being bullied on the bus please refer to the section in the next chapter which covers exactly that.

Fact Two – A school is not treated as being negligent when it comes to bullying if they were unaware that the bullying was taking place.

They have to be made aware of it first or it has to be obvious that bullying is taking place for example, incidents were witnessed by teachers. This is only fair when you think about it. How can you be responsible for your child being victimised if you were unaware that it was happening? The answer is that you can't be and nor should you be. In the interest of fairness the same even handedness has to be applied to schools.

The minute the school are made aware of it and have been given enough time to act they are liable.

Need2Know

The Difference Between Primary School Versus Secondary School Bullying

If your child is being bullied at primary school it's best if you approach their class teacher initially. As someone who works with your child on a daily basis, they will be the ones best positioned to sort out any problems between pupils. If you are not satisfied with their response then go to the head.

For secondary school bullying arranging a meeting with your child's guidance teacher, the head teacher or his or her deputy is best.

Equipping Yourself with the Facts

Before you approach the school it's best to be prepared. You will need:

- A copy of your school's anti-bullying policy. The school have to provide this to any parent who asks by law, so phone up the school secretary and ask for a copy. Having it to hand will ensure you know exactly how the school has said it will act in the circumstances and you can demand that they follow it to the letter.

- Remember the burden of proof is on you to prove that the bullying is taking place. Get details of the harassment that's taken place. Where and when did it happen? Who were the perpetrators/witnesses? Does your child have any proof like bruises or torn clothes? Be exact about everything and take notes. There's no point in saying that your son had his head shoved down the toilet once and not being able to specify when this happened. If your child has written down details this can be useful, as can emails they have sent to friends about what's been happening.

- Have exact details of how this has affected your child. Have they developed a terror of going to school/started wetting the bed? Have their grades gone down dramatically? Have they received medical attention? One mother I spoke to had to give her son something to help him sleep when he developed insomnia. It's details like these that illicit action from schools.

What Action Can the School Take?

There is a raft of measures that schools can take. These include:

- Increasing supervision in areas where bullies are most likely to strike.

- Supervising the bully.

- Speaking to the bully and their parents. This will most likely happen after a letter has been sent out to his or her parents requesting their son/ daughter's presence at the school.

- Issuing a full warning to the bully. This will include details of the penalty if the harassment of a fellow pupil doesn't cease.

- Some schools have schemes whereby the bully is asked to explain their actions to their victim with an adult present. Being made to face up to what they're doing may shame them into stopping.

- Detention.

- Internal exclusion within school. Say your son is being bullied and he's on the football team, the bully could face being unable to play on the team unless he modifies his behaviour.

- Suspension from school for a set period.

- Being expelled. This will only be used as a last resort and in extreme cases.

The Ins and Outs of Your Meeting at the School

You've made that appointment and now it's time to get down to the nitty gritty.

Should I take my child with me?

It depends on the child. How do they feel about it? If they feel awkward about being there then don't force them to be. You can always get them to write a letter about what's been happening and how it's making them feel. Tip - If they feel able to be there it may be best to speak to the school and get your child the morning or afternoon before the meeting off school. That way they won't have to be excused from class in front of the bullies if they are classmates of theirs.

Should I take someone with me?

Two heads are better than one. Both parents should be there if possible. If that is impossible then have a suitable adult deputise for the missing parent. Have a witness to the proceedings.

What proof do I need?

Bring any evidence you have for example a doctor's note or a schoolbook that the bullies have defaced. Showing the school bruises your child has or a ruined piece of clothing can be very effective.

Can I ask for more supervision for my child or the bully?

If bullying is happening in the changing rooms, in the corridors or playground then ask for supervision to be increased. If the school says it does not have the resources then explain that you are not expecting every child to receive increased supervision, only the bully.

Should I take notes of what is said?

Yes do. You may be too stressed at the time to fully take in what is being said, which is why notes are essential. You can look back on them later.

How can I make sure the school do as they've promised?

Make sure you know exactly what action they have promised to take. Get a timeline. When will they do as they've promised? Get everything in writing and make sure details of the meeting are put in your child's file.

How do I keep the line of communication open?

The last thing you want is to go to all that time and effort to visit the school and tell them about the bullying only for them to forget about it. To prevent that from happening know when and whom to contact to get an update on what they've done. You also need to know who to speak to so you can tell them whether their measures have stopped the bullying. If they haven't, you can ask them to take a different approach.

What do I do in the meantime?

Get your child to keep a bully diary. I can't stress the importance of this. You need well-documented examples.

How do I get the school to do something without becoming a pest?

The most important thing to do is *not to let the school off the hook*. Keep writing to them, phoning them up and asking for further meetings. Make a nuisance of yourself. Who cares if they have you down as a bit of a pest? Getting the bullying to cease is all that you want.

What to Say

Too often schools don't take bullying seriously. What can you as a parent say to ensure that they do?

Psychologist Cassandra Rogers offers tips on what to say to illicit action –

Don't start by blaming the school and saying 'you should be doing this/you should be doing that.' Coming across as confrontational won't help anyone least alone your child. You're there to complain about bullying not to bully.

Play on the emotional angle. Use descriptive and emotive language to describe the effects of the bullying. Tell the school about the times your child wakes you up screaming. Highlight the alienation your child feels. An example could be 'I read my child's diary and she said she felt so alone that she wanted to kill herself.'

Be polite but assertive making sure the school knows in no uncertain terms that the bullying has to stop, but make it a matter of 'we can do this' and not 'you will do this.' Nobody likes to be dictated to.

The School Says . . .

Schools aren't always as quick to admit their failings as we'd like. Quite often they trot out the same old excuses. Be prepared for them.

1. 'This school operates a no blame bullying policy.'

This means that rather than blame the bully the school prefers to try and get them to see the error of their ways using their peers. This no blame policy might seem weak to some parents, because let's face it, when your child is being bullied you have every right to be angry with the bully, but this seven pronged approach has met with some success.

Ask to see the policy the school has and if you are not satisfied by what it says the school will do, insist that you would prefer it if this situation was handled a different way. For example the bully was made to realise that their actions won't be tolerated, rather than being allowed to come to that conclusion themselves.

2. 'The person you say bullied your child has a good school record and comes from a good family.'

This panders to the myth that most bullies are delinquents. Your reaction could be 'I'm not saying they're not smart and come from a dysfunctional family, just that they are bullying my child.'

3. 'There is no bullying problem at this school.'

I call this the ostrich manoeuvre where the school would rather bury its head in the sand than admit that there's a problem. The best thing to do here is not to get into an argument, but to merely state that your child is being bullied and that's a problem to you and should be to the school.

4. 'Your child is over sensitive.'

Usually this plays along the lines of 'there's no bullying from what I can see' 'just a bit of mucking around' or 'good natured banter.' You have to be calm at this point even although inside your head you're probably screaming at what's been said. Explain calmly and rationally that you know the difference between the kidding on that goes on between children and the kind of bullying that reduces your child to tears and makes them have maudlin thoughts.

Summing Up . . .

When we send our children off to school we think they are going into a safe environment where they can learn. Discovering otherwise means that we have to revise that view and do something to get the bullying to stop.

Depending on the school that can be an easy process or an almighty struggle that will have you in despair. Never fear though because help is at hand. Schools have bullying policies and by law they have to implement them.

If they fail in that duty of care to your child there are other things you can do. See Chapter 7 to find other avenues you can go down to get the help you need.

Chapter 7:
Other Help You Can Get

You've told the school about the bullying and they've 'done what they can.' Hopefully the measures they have taken will have worked and your child will be back to their good old selves, but what if the bullying has continued?

Don't despair because the school isn't your only chance of resolving the situation.

Bullying Outside School

We have already looked at the fact that schools may refuse to take any responsibility for the bullying your child suffers out of school because legally they are not duty bound to do anything. So what then if the bullying takes place on the school bus or anywhere deemed to be outside school property?

Of course you should tell the school about the bullying that's happening on the bus and anywhere else for that matter, although strictly speaking they may not feel compelled to do anything about it. It varies from school to school whether they act. If a school takes bullying seriously they will at the very least look into the matter and may even put teachers on bus duty or at the school gates to supervise pupils. If they refuse to, point out that the school is meant to look after its pupils because it has a moral responsibility to do so.

. . . the school is meant to look after its pupils because it has a moral responsibility to do so.

Bullying on the School Bus

You should approach the bus company and inform them of what's going on. The last thing that any bus company wants is to have the bad publicity of child passengers being injured on one of their buses, especially if they need the school's contracts as many of them do. They also don't want the driver to have any distractions whilst they are driving.

What the bus company can do:

- They may insist that teachers ride on the bus if there is bullying on it or they will stop doing the bus run.

- Inform the police and say that they will use CCTV evidence to ensure that children who misbehave are prosecuted.

- If there is a community police officer they may ask them to come onto the bus to speak to pupils.

- They can even withdraw the pass that the bully has if they find out they are harassing people on the bus.

- In severe cases they may opt to stop driving children from a particular school if the bullying problem is so bad. One bus company I read about did that when pupils tried to shove a boy out the emergency exit of the bus whilst it was still moving.

- If the Local Education Authority rather than a public bus service provides the bus, you can complain to them too and ask that your child be seated near to the driver. Be warned, although this may stop bullying on the bus requesting this may set your child apart from other children as well as taking them away from their friends. It may be best to find an alternative way to get them to school even if it means driving them there yourself, or asking someone you know who does the school run to drive your children with theirs.

Talking to the Bully's Parents

In an ideal world it would be a case of knocking on the child's parents' door and telling them what's been going on. They'd be horrified at their child's behaviour and vow to put a stop to it as you sipped tea from their best china whilst seated on their sofa and nibbling on a digestive biscuit.

Sadly this is far from an ideal world and you may find that the parents of bullies insist that their little perfect princess or prince 'wouldn't do that' and 'oh your child must be *over sensitive* to mistake a little leg pulling for bullying.'

There are certain things you have to take into account before you even consider approaching the parents directly.

Do you know them well enough to have a friendly chat?

What kind of people are they? Are they reasonable? If they have a bad reputation you're best steering clear.

Can you trust yourself to control your temper and not be confrontational?

If you can't, don't go. Getting into an argument will be of no help to anyone.

Are you the kind of person who is frank or are you someone who has difficulty in getting your point across?

If you're a bit of an introvert you could end up feeling like you've been run over by a steamroller in any conversation you have with the bully's parents.

. . . you may find that the parents of bullies insist that their little perfect princess or prince 'wouldn't do that' and 'oh your child must be over sensitive to mistake a little leg pulling for bullying.'

Will you be able to explain calmly and clearly what has been happening without making any judgements?

You have to be able to put yourself in the other parents' shoes. If someone came round to your house shouting the odds and accusing your child of picking on other kids you would go on the defensive too. If they calmly explained what had been going on you would be more inclined to want to get to the bottom of it as much as them.

Would it be better if you were to meet the parents in a meeting organised by the school?

That way it would be in a controlled and monitored environment that you and they would be less likely to find intimidating.

Meet the Parents

If you feel that going ahead and speaking to the bully's parents is the best course of action, you have to be careful about how you go about it and what you say:

- Plan exactly what you are going to say. Go there and um and ah and you'll get nowhere. You have to take control of the situation.

- Don't go alone. If both parents are present there's more chance of a successful resolution.

- Don't just barge into their house. If possible contact them first by phone or pop round asking for a suitable time to chat.

- Don't be confrontational. This includes no demanding to see the 'bully.' One of the main reasons that people shouldn't approach bully's parents directly is because too often it ends with the parents at each other's throats and can even lead to violence.

- Empathise with them and the situation they find themselves in. Think of how you would feel if you were told your child was a bully. They may have no indication of what their child has been up to. Don't be surprised if they tell you that their child has suffered from bullying too because often bullied children go onto bully themselves.

- Expect them to go on the defensive. Wouldn't you if someone came over to your house and told you that your child was bullying other children?

- Listen to what they have to say and don't talk over the top of them. The key to a successful resolution is good communication.

- Try and come to some kind of decision about what's going to happen.

- If the talks are fruitless make sure that they know that you will still press ahead with getting the bullying to stop under your own steam.

- Try and keep the lines of communication open. Give them your telephone number and ensure they know they can call you.

- If the situation looks as though it may be set to get violent leave immediately.

Find Out if any other Children are being Bullied at the School

- They always say that there's more strength in numbers and they are right. If you find out that other children are being bullied meet with their parents. Together you can demand the school takes action.

- Find out if there is a bullying culture at the school. You could place an advert with a PO box number in your local paper or put an advert in the library. Word of mouth is good too. Make sure that everyone knows that what they tell you will be treated in the strictest of confidence.

Does Your School have a PTA or a Board of Governors?

You feel like you've hit a brick wall with the school, but do you know any of the PTA members/governors? Find out and bring the matter up with them.

Go to the Head's Boss

I have a friend who goes right to the top to complain about bad service or products she pays for and always with satisfying results.

- In the case of a school failing in its duty to stop your child being bullied you can go over the school's head and write to the Local Education Authority.

- You can also contact the education welfare officer there and explain the situation to them asking them to intervene. If you're unhappy with their response, contact the Local Government Ombudsman who can look at the LEA's role in dealing with your complaint. Ask your local council for details. Websites and contact details are included at the back of this book.

- Contact the Education Minister at Westminster.

Contact the Police

If your child has been assaulted it's imperative that you go to the police because whoever is responsible has committed a crime.

- Even if your child has no willing witnesses having a talking to from one of the men in blue has been known to stop bullying.

- Having their involvement will also help in your case against the bully because they will have a record of being called out that you can use.

- In severe cases you can try and take out an order banning the bully or bullies from coming within close proximity to your child. You will need substantial proof of bullying to convince a judge.

Getting Your Local Councillor/MP Involved

Go to your councillor or MP's local surgery. Alternatively you can write to them and request a meeting.

Write to the Children's Commissioners

Wales were the first to appoint one but there are also individual ones for children in England (there the post is called the Minister for Children), Scotland and Northern Ireland. Contact details are at the back of this book.

The Legal Route

This is not to be recommended, as it's very rare that a case succeeds and it's also a very long drawn out and expensive process that can go on for years. You will also need an abundance of evidence to prove the school was aware of what was going on and failed to act.

Evidence could include a doctor's letter, details of school and police involvement, a report from an educational psychologist on the effects of the bullying etc.

The first step is to speak to a lawyer who will talk you through what they can and cannot do and the likelihood of a successful lawsuit. If you are on a low income you may get Legal Aid.

If this all sounds too daunting a prospect you may find that simply getting a lawyer's letter sent to the school may stir them into taking some action.

Use the Media

Tell your story and this may shame the school into doing something. Your best bet is to contact your local newspaper. There should be a telephone number that you can call the news desk on.

Be warned - they will want to send round a photographer and speak to your child.

Threaten to Take Your Child Out of School

This is the last resort. Speak to the school about it. This may spur them into doing more.

If it doesn't, there are two options open to you –

Find another school

- Contact the head teacher of the school that you want your child to go to and see if there are any places available.

- Ask to come in and speak to them directly so that you can explain about the problems you are having at your child's other school.

- Find out what their bullying policy is and how effective it is. If the head doesn't seem to be that forthcoming then be wary of sending your child to that school. Remember most schools that deny they have a bullying problem are usually the ones that are worst hit.

Teach your child at home

Sometimes parents feel that the best thing to do is to teach their children at home.

Before you commit yourself to teaching your child at home look at the practicalities. Most importantly do you have the time? Is there a place where your child can work? How will it impact upon the rest of the household?

For more in depth advice about home schooling see the *Help List* at the back of this book.

Summing Up . . .

You've been to the school and still the bullying carries on:

- Know that you have other options and so does your child.

- Ensure that they know that, because children who are being bullied can slip into despair. They may be upset to find that telling you about the bullying hasn't allowed you to wave a magic wand and get the bullies to just disappear.

Chapter 8:
Inside the Mind of the Bullied Child

We've looked at stopping the bullying in the previous two chapters, but that isn't all that we can do. There are other ways to help our damaged children and we can make a start on that in this chapter.

We first have to fully understand how bullying has affected them, including the thought processes that children go through when they are bullied and what the after effects are of the inner turmoil they go through. Once we fully understand that we are more capable of empathising with them and helping them to come to terms with what has happened to them and to undo the damage.

The Different Stages that the Bullied Child Goes Through

Bullied children go through a whole raft of emotions and they are all negative ones that are turned inwards on themselves. That's why bullying is so psychologically damaging.

Bullied children go through a whole raft of emotions and they are all negative ones that are turned inwards on themselves. That's why bullying is so psychologically damaging.

The Mental Process

- **Disbelief** – They can't believe that this is really happening to them.

- **Denial** – They feel that it can't be happening to them. That they must be imagining it or being over sensitive.

- **Realisation** – This is happening.

- **Blame** – They blame themselves thinking they must have done something to cause/deserve it or it wouldn't be happening.

- **Anger** – They become angry with themselves.

- **Shame** – They feel ashamed that they have 'allowed' this to happen.

- **Isolation** – 'Now I've been marked out as different and everybody will know.'

- **Terror** - Constant fear that it's going to happen again.

The psychological effects of bullying run deep, leaving mental scars.

The Psychological Scars

It's no wonder with the turmoil that bullied children go through often on a daily basis that the psychological effects of bullying run deep, leaving mental scars. Unlike physical scars these take a long time to heal and sometimes in extreme cases will never fully heal. I can vouch for that.

It wasn't being punched in the stomach that hurt me the most when I became the target of a particularly vicious teenage boy when I was at school. It was having one of his gang who targeted me, striding up to me on the school bus and spitting *'ugly'* in my face in front of everyone. Even today I am very insecure about my looks. That happened about sixteen years ago now and I still remember it like it was yesterday. Sometimes I even think I can even feel the spittle on my face as my tormentor screamed his insult at me.

That's one of the main things that parents may not realise about bullying when it's their child on the receiving end. That it's not just a matter of feeling like rubbish when it's happening, but the effects can be long lasting. Your child may look like they're doing okay, but inside it may be a different story.

Of course I'm an adult now and supposedly older and wiser, maybe I should be able to brush all of the insults and blows I took under the carpet, but somehow I'm not quite there yet. If I feel this bad sixteen years on when the bullying is half a lifetime away, just think how bad your child may feel if they are being tormented now.

Why the Effects of Bullying Never End

Being bullied strikes right at the core of who you are. You believe that there is something wrong with you. There has to be because what's happening to you isn't happening to everyone else. You are the one who makes you different, so it must be you.

If you ask most people who have suffered from bullying in their lives they will tell you the same thing, that it's the mental effects of bullying that stay with them. This may be down to the fact that broken bones and cuts heal, but wounds to the psyche run deeper and are hidden, no one can see them so they are less easy to deal with.

Why Bullying can Cause so much Psychological Harm

Psychologists believe that each individual is a product of their environment and experiences. If you are someone who lives in an environment of fear where you are being made to feel small, that experience starts to mould you, making you do things that you otherwise wouldn't do, if you weren't being bullied.

. . . broken bones and cuts heal, but wounds to the psyche run deeper and are hidden, no one can see them so they are less easy to deal with.

- You may start to walk with your head down and back bent, terrified of making eye contact with anyone, because you become convinced that it's you looking at the bully or coming across as cocky that starts it off. You may think that someone will see you as challenging them and start picking on you because of it.

- You may stop answering questions in class because 'swots' always get bullied.

- You may stop going out with your friends and become reclusive because you are worried that you might bump into your tormentors.

- You may become jumpy and paranoid that the bully is going to start on you today, putting you in a constant state of alarm even when nothing is happening.

- You might find yourself being conditioned to behave in a certain way that you feel will lessen your chance of being bullied that day. It probably won't so you despair of it ever ending.

The reason this happens and victims of bullying modify their behaviour in reaction to what's happening to them is down to one thing. *They blame themselves for the bullying and believe that if they modify their behaviour it will stop.* When this doesn't work they turn all of that anger inward. Again it's their fault that they're being bullied. They should have nipped it in the bud. They should stand up for themselves. Notice, it's all on them and not the bully.

My Experience

Everything that I did when I was being bullied was governed by what was happening. How I walked. How and when I talked – I have a speech impediment which means that I can't pronounce the letter 'r' and 'l' properly, something that I inherited from my mother. This caused a great deal of hilarity amongst my peers (even when many of them couldn't string two words together) and no small amount of embarrassment to me. I lived in constant fear even when I got a brief respite from the bullying. It would happen at school, on the bus and outside my home. Nowhere was safe and even if it was, I didn't feel safe.

Adult Bully Survivors

To truly understand how bullying can have such long lasting effects the best people to talk to are adult bully survivors. These are people who have been there and know what it's like.

'Many years ago now I was bullied at secondary school and so ashamed that I couldn't tell anyone, not even my parents. It left me wishing that I had never been born. Even now there are days when I think about what happened to me and feel the same way.'

Simon

'The bullying I suffered took many forms. It started off as name calling and being sent to Coventry by the group of girls I used to hang about with who turned against me. Then it escalated to the point where I was being hit with books and people's fists almost every day at school. I used to be a happy child with a lot of spirit, but that was soon knocked out of me. That was thirty years ago and I am now a complete introvert. I have no friends and only my children and husband keep me going.'

Cathy

'I lost a piece of me when I was repeatedly bullied over two years and I never got it back. My parents got the bullying to stop by taking it up with the school and pestering them, but the effects still remain. People don't realise that once the spirit is taken out of you it's difficult to get it back. I never have, but I have friends who were bullied who seem to be okay now. You never can tell though.'

Anne

'What I suffered made me feel so bad that I used to hurt myself in an attempt to get out of going to school. I would shove my hand down my throat and make myself sick, punch myself in the stomach and then complain of tummy ache. Once I even threw myself down stairs. My parents just thought I was clumsy. They never asked why. I don't have any kind of relationship with them now. I feel that they betrayed me by not cottoning on to what was happening.'

Kirsty

'Bullying at school has led to me becoming so meek that I get bullied at work too. I feel so weak and relive the hell every day in flashbacks. When it happens people look at me like I'm schizophrenic.'

Irene

Bullied Children's Fears

Bullied children fear many things:

- They will always be bullied.

- They'll never make friends again.

- They'll always carry the stigma of being bullied.

- They'll be labelled a grass if they tell about the bullying.

- That the insults the bullies sling at them are true.

- The bullying will never end.

How to get Your Child to Express their Feelings

Bottling up feelings is detrimental to anyone. You need your child to open up something, which may not be easy.

- Try some role-playing where you replay incidents of bullying and switch roles. This gets them to express their feelings and helps you to understand how it feels.

- If they can't talk to you get them an appointment with a school guidance teacher or your family GP and perhaps they will be able to talk to them.

- Ask them to write down things that have happened in a poem, short story or an essay. Even if they don't want to show it to you, putting your thoughts down on paper helps our brains to digest them. For younger children ask them to draw you a picture.

Things that Helped Me . . .

From the Mouths of the Bullied

I learnt a technique later in life that I wished I'd used when I was being bullied that you may find useful too:

- I'd write down details of a negative experience that had happened to me as soon as I could get the time to do it.

- I'd write down how it made me feel.

- Later I would analyse the situation and say to myself 'if I told someone about what had happened how would they interpret it?'

- Second time round, I found that I'd interpret the incident completely differently and more positively than I did initially.

This method is particularly good for the bullied child because often when bullying happens they respond by thinking negatively about themselves rather than the bully.

For example, for a bullied child the incident could be –

> *'I was picked on today by the bully who punched me. This was my fault because I shouldn't have smiled.'*

Looking at the incident later the child may write:

> *'Everyone has a right to smile if they want. The person who hit me is nothing but a coward and a bully.'*

Tip – You can help your child with this exercise or even do it verbally although this is best if it's written down as writing has proven to be very therapeutic.

Things That Helped Me...

> *'I write stories where I'm a superhero and I get to beat up all the bad guys.'*
>
> ***James (10)***

> *'My parents believing me helped me more than I thought it ever could. Just knowing that they knew how I felt and that I could share things with them made me feel like a great weight had been lifted off of me.'*
>
> ***Callie (15)***

> *'I took up kickboxing. Using a punch bag and pretending it was the thug who had beaten upon me for two years made me feel strong.'*
>
> ***Darren (16)***

Summing Up . . .

By far the worst effects of bullying are the psychological effects. Helping your child to overcome them is vital to their recovery.

In the next chapter I will suggest ways that you can help your child to improve their shattered self-esteem. This is just as important as getting the bullying to stop.

Chapter 9:
Boosting Your Child's Self-esteem

You can always spot a bullied child. They are the ones walking with their head down to avoid making direct eye contact and their shoulders hunched. Their backs are all tense and every movement can seem like it takes great effort. They have cripplingly low self-esteem.

Why Self-esteem is Important

Self-esteem is something that we all need because if we don't feel good about ourselves than nobody else will. Self-esteem makes us believe that we can do things. In a child that's vital to help them flourish and to grow into the happy, confident adults we know they are capable of being.

A child with good self-esteem will be focused and enjoy life greeting every day as a new challenge.

A child with poor self-esteem will have little sense of direction and be miserable with every day being seen as something to dread.

You can always spot a bullied child. They are the ones walking with their head down to avoid making direct eye contact and their shoulders hunched.

Repairing Damaged Self-esteem

The good news is that it is possible to make your child walk tall again although it will take time, patience and a whole lot of perseverance, but it will be worth it in the end. Think of self-esteem as a stack of bricks. Bullying takes away some of those bricks and they come toppling down. In order to get the self-esteem back you have to start rebuilding that wall and the only way to do that is a brick at a time.

Confidence Building Exercises

Try rebuilding your child's shattered self-esteem using a series of confidence building exercises. The aim of these exercises is to make your child feel good about themselves again.

Please remember, part of having confidence is feeling that you have the right to say no. For that reason the participation of your child in these exercises because they want to is vital. They won't have the desired effect if they feel that they have to do them to please you. Make sure that they know why you are doing this for their benefit and not for yours.

Exercise One

Help give them a sense of worth

Children who have undergone some kind of psychological trauma such as bullying tend to have a distorted view of themselves and their worth. In this exercise we help them to see themselves as the wonderful human beings they truly are by highlighting their good points.

- Ask them to do two columns. One with the heading 'personality' and the other with 'appearance.' Note – I know that we should be stressing that it's the inside that counts, but no one wants to think of themselves as ugly and that's how bullied children often think about themselves.

- Now ask them to write down what they like about themselves under both categories. This can be anything from saying they are kind to saying they have nice hair.

What to expect:

- They will probably feel negative about both aspects of themselves.

- If they seem stuck help them out. Say something along the lines of 'you are always helping your sister with her homework, that makes you kind.'

- Think about what they are good at and incorporate those things in the personality column. Are they the one who always waters the plants when you forget? Do they cheer everyone else up when they are feeling down? Do they look after their younger siblings? Anything goes here, as long as it makes them think positively about themselves.

Once they've finished:

- Take a look at what they have written (it may be best to do it whilst they are out of the room in case they get embarrassed).

- Go through the list and discuss every good point they have written adding in things that you think should be there and giving examples to back it up. This will help them to imprint them in their mind.

- Stress that the good points they have picked up about themselves are also how others see them and that they shouldn't listen to anyone who says otherwise especially their tormentors.

Exercise Two

Encourage social interaction

Bullied children tend to want to hide themselves away, so encourage them to take up a new hobby that involves as least one other person. This encourages them to socially interact instead of making them awkward as many bullied children are.

This could mean -

- Taking up karate or another martial art. This will have the dual role of making them feel better about defending themselves if the occasion arises, and will also help them to make new friends, including ones who may have had the shared experience of having been bullied.

- Joining a dance class. And no, this isn't just for girls.

- Taking up a musical instrument. Finding or developing a new talent helps build self-esteem as well as keeping them busy and giving them less chance to think.

- Getting singing lessons. What child hasn't fantasised about being a pop star? Look in your local paper for singing teachers. They may not be as expensive as you think.

- Is there a youth theatre or acting workshops specifically aimed at children near you? Acting is great for helping to bring children out of themselves and youth theatre/workshops offers the perfect friendly environment.

- If your child is so shy that sending them to a class is out of the question then why not just try inviting one or two of their friends around? This way they get to have fun in a safe environment and their pals may return the favour and invite them over to theirs.

Exercise Three

Alter what happened to them

After each encounter with a bully, the victim often wishes that they could have handled the situation better. With this exercise they get to do exactly that – in their head or on paper.

Here's how it's done –

- Your child writes down details of an incident that happened. Perhaps the bully let forth with a stream of abuse whilst others looked on and your child's face crumpled. Or maybe the bully tripped them up and they went flying as everyone howled with laughter.

- They write down what they would have liked to have said or done. For the above example it could be that they laughed and said out loud 'Hey what's his problem?' The tripping incident could involve making a quip about 'taking a trip.' Disarming the bully with humour and making lookers on laugh with you rather than at you is an excellent tool.

Tip - The knack of this exercise is to come up with solutions that make them feel better without them turning into a bully themselves, so no physical violence. The whole point of this exercise is to show your child that they can turn the tables on the bully without copying their anti-social behaviour.

Exercise Four

Help them to come up with their own happy song

This will be a song that makes them feel happy no matter where they are. They can hum it in their head for an instant happy feeling. Confide in them what yours is.

Tips for choosing the song –

- It can be a chart topper that you could pay for them to have downloaded as a ring tone onto their mobile.

- The song may be one that made them happy when they were little, perhaps one that you used to sing to them that has good memories.

- The song could be connected to a happy time in their lives say a family wedding or maybe their favourite film.

- If they can't think of one have a look together. You could do this on the Internet, go into a music store and let them listen to some tunes or talk about their favourite films and theme tunes.

Exercise Five

Help them to feel good about themselves

Ask them to make a list of the things they don't like about themselves. Then they have to turn every thing they don't like about themselves into something a bit more positive with your help.

For example, if they say that they hate the way they are terrified of going to school every day and they feel like a coward for being scared, you could write in the opposite column, you are proud that despite how terrified they are they still went to school, which shows they have guts.

Tips:

- Suggest that they carry this list around with them to look at when they feel blue. If they are worried about someone seeing it suggest that they memorise it instead.

- They could try using the good things about themselves as positive affirmations to be repeated last thing at night or first thing in the morning. For example they could look in the mirror while they're brushing their teeth and say 'I have a nice smile.' Saying that will make them smile.

Exercise Six

Do fun things together

This is what I call the Happy Stuff exercise.

- Draw up a list and get your child to choose one thing every day to do.

- The list could include things like watching an episode of their favourite show, playing a family board game or computer game together, having a family karaoke competition, going on a family day trip anywhere they want or taking them shopping for something they want.

Exercise Seven

Treat your child like an adult whenever you can

- This could mean getting them involved in the decision making in the house or in adult type activities like cooking or gardening.

- Talk to them as if they are another adult not a child and respect their views no matter how much you don't agree with them. This will show that you respect and trust them.

- Always ensure that you make good eye contact and give them your full attention. Think of how you feel when you are talking to someone and are acutely aware of the fact they are not listening to you. Your child shouldn't have to feel that way.

Exercise Eight

Teach your child how to walk tall

Good posture makes you look and feel confident.

Try this –

Get them to stand with their feet together. Now ask them to pull their shoulders back and upwards. Then to pull in their tummy muscles. Hey presto we have instant confidence.

Tip - Turn it into a fun exercise by pretending to be a catwalk model to illustrate. Play music if it helps.

Other Things You Can Do:

- Say something positive every time they make a negative comment about themselves. Be wary that they are not copying your negative language. Negativity is often passed down from parent to child.

- Stop them from using phrases like 'I can't,' 'I'm not good at' and 'I hate myself when . . .' Make them aware when they are using them. Don't use them for yourself either.

- Be there to listen whenever they want to talk even if it means letting them send you a text message when they're in school.

- Do fun things together, not necessarily as parent and child but as friends.

- Always give them something to look forward to. This can be a trip to somewhere they enjoy, or a CD they want.

- Try and provide them with a stress free home. This will help them to feel that their home is a haven and not somewhere that they have to hide from even more tension.

- Make sure they realise you have confidence in them. This in turn will give them confidence in themselves. Say things like 'thank you,' 'please,' 'you'd be doing be a big favour if you helped me with the dishes' and 'I'm proud of you.'

- Try not to get angry. This may trigger bad memories about the bullying. Instead be rational and calm and explain why you are upset. This could be something like 'I'm upset that your room isn't tidy, because I want you to have a nice room with nice things.'

Summing Up . . .

- Your child's confidence has taken one all mighty knock, but it is possible to build it back up a step at a time.

- Do it as a team and involve the whole family.

- Just think of self-esteem and confidence as a bridge that has been knocked down. It can and will be rebuilt. Believe that and your child will too.

Bullying: A Parent's Guide
Help List

As well as offering information and advice to parents, children can also benefit from speaking to trained counsellors about their experiences so contact details and web sites for them to visit are also listed.

Advisory Centre for Education (ACE)

An independent advice centre for parents, offering information about state education in England and Wales for 5-16 year olds. They offer free telephone advice.

Advice lines open Monday - Friday 2-5pm - freephone: 0808 800 5793.

Exclusion information line: 020 7704 9822

Overseas callers, please call: 00 44 20 7704 3397 (General)
or 00 44 20 7704 3398 (Exclusion)

www.ace-ed.org.uk

Anti-Bullying Campaign

10 Borough High Street, London SE1 9QQ

Tel: 020 7378 1446 (10:00 - 16:00)

Bullying Online

Invaluable online help and advice for parents tackling bullying including a problem page for parents. They have a full section on advice for parents and for pupils on what steps to take to stop bullying including legal action.

www.bullying.co.uk

Careline

Telephone counselling for anyone experiencing bullying or other problems.

London: 020 8514 1177

Leeds: 0532 302 226

ChildLine

Children's charity ChildLine offers a free 24-hour helpline for children in distress or danger. Trained volunteer counsellors comfort, advise and protect children and young people who may feel they have nowhere else to turn. They also have information sheets online you can print out, as well as a comprehensive list of contact numbers for ChildLine offices throughout the UK.

www.childline.org.uk

Tel: 0800 1111 (for children to call)

Address: ChildLine, Freepost NATN1111, London E1 6BR

Childline Scotland

www.childline.org.uk/Scotland.asp

Free bullying helpline: 0800 44 11 11 (3.30 - 9.00pm)

Childline Scotland, Freepost1111, Glasgow G1 1BR

Children's Commissioners

England

Beverley Hughes (officially called The Minister for Children)

Email: haywoodmw@parliament.uk

Tel: 020 7219 3000

Margaret Hodge MP, House of Commons, London SW1A 0AA

Northern Ireland

Nigel Williams

www.niccy.org

Email: info@niccy.org

NICCY, Millennium House, 17-25 Great Victoria Street, Belfast BT2 7BN

Tel: (028) 9031 1616

Scotland

Kathleen Marshall

www.cypcommissioner.org/content/about-us/index.php

Email: enquiries@cypcommissioner.org

Commissioner for Children and Young People in Scotland, 85 Holyrood Road, Edinburgh EH8 8AU

Tel: 0131 718 6404

Wales

Peter Clarke

www.childcom.org.uk

Oystermouth House, Charter Court, Phoenix Way, Llansamlet, Swansea SA7 9FS

Tel: 01792 765600

Fax: 01792 765601

Email: post@childcomwales.org.uk

Children's Commissioner for Wales, Penrhos Manor, Oak Drive, Colwyn Bay, Conwy LL29 7YW

Tel: 01492 523333

Fax: 01492 523336

post@childcomwales.org.uk

The Children's Legal Centre

Legal advice covering all aspects of the law affecting children and young people. This service is open to children and parents.

www.childrenslegalcentre.com

The Children's Legal Centre, Wivenhoe Park, University of Essex, Colchester, Essex CO4 3SQ

DfES website on bullying

Government website with the slogan 'Don't Suffer in Silence.' Also behind first ever anti-bullying week that had massive press coverage and celebrity endorsement. They do an anti-bullying pack.

www.dfes.gov.uk/bullying

Contact: Improving Behaviour and Attendance Division, Department for Education and Employment, Sanctuary Buildings, Great Smith Street, London SW1P 3BT

Tel: 0870 000 2288

Email: anti.bullying@dfes.gsi.gov.uk

Home schooling information:

Education Otherwise

A UK-based membership organisation which provides support and information for parents who home school their children.

www.education-otherwise.org

The Home Education Advisory Advisory Service

A national home education charity.

www.heas.org.uk

Home Education

www.home-education.org.uk

The frequently answered questions section is particularly helpful.

Kidscape

National charity that's been helping to eradicate bullying and child abuse for twenty years.

www.kidscape.org.uk

Kidscape, 2 Grosvenor Gardens, London SW1W 0DH.

Tel: 020 7730 3300

Fax: 020 7730 7081

Helpline: 08451 205 204

Local Government Ombudsman

If you have a complaint about the education that your child is receiving and your local education authority doesn't deal with it in the manner you think they should, the ombudsman is the person you contact.

England

There are three in England. Check the website for details.

www.lgo.org.uk

Scotland

www.scottishombudsman.org.uk

Scottish Public Services Ombudsman, 4 Melville Street, Edinburgh EH3 7NS

Tel: 0870 011 5378
Fax: 0870 011 5379
Email: enquiries@scottishombudsman.org.uk

Wales

www.ombudsman-wales.org

Northern Ireland

www.ni-ombudsman.org.uk

Parentline Plus

A charity that offers advice to anyone parenting a child.

www.parentlineplus.org.uk

Tel: 0808 800 2222

Especially for Kids

There are a host of web sites for children as well as sections in the sites listed above all presenting solid advice in an understandable way. Here are some of the most child friendly.

Antibully Website

Advice for children on how to tackle bullies presented in an attractive way.

www.antibully.org.uk

Bully Free Zone

Bully Free Zone was established in 1996 to provide a service for children and young people who had issues around bullying. There is also a section for parents.

www.ichameleon.co.uk/bfz/kids/helpimbeingbullied.htm

Let's Beat the Bullies

This is a site created by children of Whickham School and Gateshead City Learning Centre, which gives an insight into bullying. It also has bullied children's stories so that your child will know that they are not alone. A Year Seven survival guide is included.

www.letsbeatthebullies.com

National Society for the Protection of Children

The kid's zone has brief down-to-earth advice on bullying.

www.nspcc.org.uk/homepage2/bullying.htm

Sort It

This is a great website for kids aged 11-16 which deals with issues like exam revision and technology as well as bullying. A message board is also included and is moderated so your child won't be exposed to bad language.

www.sortit.org.uk

Note – Please note websites rarely change their addresses, but contact details are subject to change at any time.

Some Useful Reading

Liberated Parents, Liberated Children

Adele Faber, Elaine Mazlish, Piccadilly Press - £8.99

The authors are internationally acclaimed, award-winning experts on parent-child communication. The book contains 'advice and examples of the countless ways the use of language can build self-esteem, inspire confidence and encourage responsibility.'

Smart Thinking: Confidence & Success Sorted

Frank McGinty, Piccadilly Press - £5.99

The author, a principal guidance teacher in a school in Glasgow believes that all children can reach their potential. In this title he helps teenagers to develop their self-belief and beat their fears. This book is ideal for children who have been bullied.

Helping Children to Build Self-esteem:
A Photocopiable Activities Book

Deborah Plummer, Jessica Kingsley Publishers - £15.95

Offering over 100 simple, practical and fun activities specifically aimed at helping children to build and maintain self-esteem that is based on the author's extensive clinical experience. It contains photocopiable activity sheets that are suitable for individuals. This unique activities book is said to be 'an invaluable resource for anyone looking for creative, enjoyable ways of helping children to build their self-esteem.'

Creating Kids Who Can

Jean Robb & Hilary Letts, Hodder & Stoughton - £6.99

Creating Kids Who Can is a practical guide for unlocking the potential of your child no matter the age or ability. It's said to be based on a ground-breaking process devised by the authors and to introduce a 'holistic and nurturing approach to learning that will help your child to develop confidently' and to also help you to understand your child.

Don't Sweat The Small Stuff for Teens

Richard Carlson, Hodder & Stoughton - £8.99

The new bestseller from the author of the Don't Sweat the Small Stuff series, gives invaluable help for the many problem areas for teenagers in a highly amusing way. Topics of the mini essays include 'Don't sweat the future,' 'Start a mutual listening club' and 'Notice your parents doing things right.'

Need2Know
Information

We hope you have found this book useful and informative.

If you would like to order further copies of this book or any of our other titles, then please give us a call or visit our website at www.n2kbooks or www.forwardpress.co.uk

Need2Know Information
Remus House
Coltsfoot Drive
Peterborough
PE2 9JX

Telephone: 01733 898105

Email: info@forwardpress.co.uk